D1504411

Prais

BE A PARENT CHAMPION:

A Guide to Becoming a Partner with Your Child's School

From a teacher, visionary and school leader for over 20 years comes the courageous truth about effective parent partnering for school success. Tovi Scruggs knows exactly what our students need from school and home to achieve. But it is her insights and strategies focused on transforming parents into champions who make their children's college dreams come true, that makes this book exceptional. Our only choice must be to carefully read Scruggs' words and follow her directions in *Parent Champion* for the benefit of our students, as we can no longer afford to simply wait on the system to do what it has never had the will to do before.

—Glenn E. Singleton

Author:

Courageous Conversations About Race: A Fieldbook for Achieving Equity in Schools and MORE Courageous Conversations About Race

Through Ms. Scruggs' efforts, I became a better parent. She was able to guide me through an often confusing and frustrating process, which allowed me to see the fruits of our labor—my daughter's high school graduation with honors and acceptance into UC Riverside. Ms. Scruggs is a definite asset and I can attest to the fact that she will bring out untapped potential and qualities in individuals and organizations that work to the greater good.

—Adilah Bilal

Parent Champion, Mother of 2

Before critiquing the current generation, we must also question and assess the generation who raised and educated it. This work of Tovi Scruggs keeps us all holistically accountable (school and family). *Parent Champion* takes the process of educational parenting out of the realm of theory and moves us into practice. This is simply a must read and a must do.

—Ammar Saheli, Ed.D, MS, PPSC

Director, San Lorenzo Unified School District

Tovi Scruggs is committed to designing empowered partnerships between homes and schools in order to ensure that our children reach their academic potential and succeed in life. The health and well being of our children and our community requires that parents are knowledgeable about and engaged in the education process. *Parent Champion* gives parents and guardians the lay of the land and grounds our expectations in a hard reality. It challenges us to be reflective and proactive. It has practical tools that are tried and tested, use one or use them all....Just get in action!

—Jenee Johnson
Parent Champion, Mother of 1
Director, San Francisco Black Infant Health Program
San Francisco Department of Public Health

As a veteran educator, I have always embraced the notion of parents as partners. *Parent Champion* is a small book with a big message—parents play a pivotal role in the academic success of their children. Rather than leave parents with just this important point, *Parent Champion* gives concrete examples of steps we can take to help cultivate the genius that lies in every child. I recommend this little gem with enthusiasm!

—Debra Watkins

Founder of CA Association of African-American Educators

Parent Champion is a life saver for parents drowning in the rough seas of educating their children. Tovi Scruggs offers concrete, practical strategies to help parents sharpen the tools needed to mold successful offspring. By helping us to hone our coaching skills with our children, *Parent Champion* helps us to create our best parent selves, thus creating our best hope for shaping the future.

—Lasha Pierce M.D.

Parent Champion, Mother of 3

I stand in awe of Tovi's honesty, determination, courage, and her commitment to student success. This book is packed with road-tested tips and real-world strategies you can start using immediately to empower parents and families as student advocates.

—Adam Taylor

Executive Director of K-12 Operations, WCCUSD

Tovi Scruggs is a life-long learner and educator. She offers are clear and direct guide for parents of traditionally under-served students. Her recommendations—based on personal experience and educational research—will be useful for *all* parents who want to act as Parent Champions and support their children so that they are able to be successful in school and life.

—Dr. Fred Brill
Superintendent, San Lorenzo USD

Parent Champion is an excellent source and tool, not only for those parents who want to become involved, but also for those that are involved but would like to be more effective. When it comes to the concept of partnerships between schools and parents, *Parent Champion* is applicable to all parents, teachers, and staff.

—Amber Hunter
Parent Champion, Mother of 4

Tovi has a deep understanding of the parent partnership required for a positive home/school relationship. The approach she describes will push parents to new levels with greater personal accountability. *Parent Champion* is an easy read with tips from personal accounts and testimonies that will inspire parents to try something new.

—Melanie Spears, Ed.D
Senior Education Specialist and CEO, Excel Consulting

As parents who did not attend college, we were still able to provide meaningful guidance to our daughter which enabled her to be a stronger student, more conscious of self, and better prepared to realize her goals as a result of following the *Parent Champion* principles. She is now in her third year at St. Mary's College of California. Though it is no easy task, the guidance outlined in this book will help you be a more powerful "Parent Champion" to your children.

—Rhonda Fortier-Bourne
Parent Champion, Mother of 2

The *Parent Champion* model provides a pattern for increased parental involvement with their child's educational, emotional, psychological, and physical well-being, all of which are necessary to become a mature adult who is a contributing member of society to the extent their ability, capacity and potential will allow. I endorse this program wholeheartedly.

—Pastor William S. Epps
Second Baptist Church, Los Angeles, CA

Ms. Scruggs, a visionary and passionate educator, has dedicated her personal life and professional career to confront and ameliorate the gaps that are holding groups of students away from meeting and exceeding their God given talents and academic potential. She ardently believes that all children can learn to the same high levels. She also knows that it will take every ounce of our collective time, talents, and resources to dramatically impact students' academic achievement. Parents and families are an integral piece of the educational success puzzle, but they are often one of the hardest groups to effectively reach. Breaking through life's distraction to get the attention of these busy adults requires a strong and effective message. Using a practical, no-nonsense approach, *Parent Champion* delivers this message with current and compelling strategies that cultivate authentic parent involvement and engagement.

Parent Champion bridges the cultural gap between schools and parents/communities, strives to advance relationships between teachers, parents and students, and identifies community resources that can be used to support students' academic success.

—Robyn Fisher

Co-Founder and Board Chair,

The Choose College Foundation, Inc.

The African American Regional Educational Alliances

BE A
PARENT CHAMPION

A Guide to Becoming a
Partner with Your Child's School

Tovi C. Scruggs

d\rt**path**
PUBLISHING

Alameda, California

Published in the United States by
Dirt Path Publishing
2201 Shoreline Avenue #2623
Alameda, California 94501

www.DirtPathPublishing.com

Exterior Design by Kenneth Bartlett-Preston
Interior Design by Carmen Klube

ISBN 978-0-615-93978-0

Manufactured in the United States of America
First Edition

This book is dedicated to all those who have the will to become champions in service to our children.

CONTENTS

ACKNOWLEDGEMENTS & GRATITUDE

First and foremost, I give ultimate gratitude to God, My Creator and My Most High, for breathing into me a purpose and vision in the larger work of education to serve our children, lead and inspire fellow educators, and create Parent Champions for the greater good of our children's success for generations to come. Without my strong conviction and faith in a support far greater than any*one* or any*thing*, I would not be where I am today doing work I love and serving others with my innate gifts and talents from a place of joy, ease, love, and flow. I am truly blessed and deeply grateful.

I am grateful for having had one of the best mothers in the entire world; she was perfect for me. She was truly a Parent Champion, instilling excellence and pride in my school work, setting up structured study time at a table free of distraction, getting me tutors when needed, investigating colleges together (when there was no Internet!), consciously nurturing my spirit, and supporting *my* dreams and vision for myself.

Thank you to my father and all of my family on all sides. I have been blessed to have direct, blended, and extended family members who value education, love me, and support me.

This book would not be possible without the vision of ASA Academy & Community Science Center, which served as a spiritual journey, leadership boot-camp, think-tank, and wonderful oasis of what is absolutely possible when parents and dynamic educators come together with a "by any means necessary" attitude and the same intention of success for our children. Thank you to ASA students and parents for teaching me so much and for trusting me to guide you to success. This book highlights much of what we learned together.

Special acknowledgement to Sharon Parker, the co-founder of ASA; we did what most only dream of. While the sacrifices were great, I know we would do it again. Thank you for being my soul-sister.

I am in gratitude to Shannette Slaughter and Terry E. Hill, dear friends who unknowingly inspired me to take action to write simply because they did.

Witnessing parts of their writing processes made authoring look doable.

If you are a teacher, you know that nothing gives you more fulfillment than seeing your students thrive. My heart is full to be able to include Kenneth Bartlett-Preston, ASA Class of 2006, in these acknowledgements for his outstanding professionalism and skills in graphic design. I love the cover, thank you.

Thank you to all of the parents and teachers of San Lorenzo High School, home of the Rebels. Thank you to my dynamic staff who is working courageously to honor our new vision. I am honored to serve as your leader. Thank you for trusting me, following me, and working with me to co-create success for our children. To the student Rebels, I love you. This book is for you.

Thank you to my most hands-on mentors Diane Bernard, Pam Wilson, and Sheryl Cambra. I hope I am making you proud and serving your legacies well.

I thank every spiritual teacher and pastor who has touched my life and blessed me with your word.

Among them, I thank Charlie Flowers, whose paramount support has kept me physically and emotionally healthy for the stamina to do this work. Special thanks goes to Pastor William S. Epps, who told me when I was 15 years old, "Service is the price you pay for the space you occupy." Thank you - that has carried me. In addition, I give gratitude to Pastors Patricia Scott-Brooks and Jenee Scott for teaching me what is simply priceless: true and direct application of spiritual principles. And, finally, I am deeply grateful to my Abba Malaku. Thank you for being a shining example of selflessness in service. Thank you for assisting me and growing me to be more of who I came here to be and modeling for me how to shine my light for good.

And this gratitude would not be complete without acknowledging the professional excellence and support from Nicole Lusiani Elliott and her team at Dirt Path Publishing. Thank you for echoing that very special "yes!" We did it!

INTRODUCTION

"If you are thinking 1 year ahead, sow seed.
If you are thinking 10 years ahead, plant a tree.
If you are thinking 100 years ahead, educate the people."
—*Kuan Tzu, Chinese Poet*

We all want our children to succeed. This book is a testament to that desire.

This book is not a traditional parenting book. This book is a *partnering* book. It is a book designed for parents to create better school success for their own children as the initial step, which will then help improve our schools to better serve our students and families on a systemic level with the spirit of oneness. It is a book serving to articulate the need for parents and educators to engage in a partnering-relationship as "we" and "us," treating and serving children as "ours."

What I am about to say may seem alarming coming from an educational leader, but I love our children and humanity enough to stand in truth and courage of what must be said: our children are not fully served as our current schools stand. School, alone, is not enough to produce the type of young person you may envision your child to become. Currently, the school system is too convoluted and teachers simply cannot do it alone. The job is too great and schools have too many distractors and competing moral values for you to trust that your child is getting exactly what you want for them.

As educators, we try—most of us—our very best to serve all children and love all children, but without the parents, the job is that much harder, overwhelming, and can feel futile. Day after day, year after year, parents continually turn their most precious possessions over to us—often without any sort of monitoring. It is imperative that parents partner with schools and take more significant and active roles in our children's education. Parents must take action in the education of our children with greater intentionality, clarity, and strategy.

I am aware that asking parents to be quality partners with schools, in turn, creates a dialogue and expectation that schools, leaders, counselors, and teachers improve in partnering as well. Good. It's not a blame-game or competition, it's an opportunity to show up more fully and partner, then nurture the greater invitation to create success for our children from there.

As a teacher, visionary, and leader with over 20 years of experience, I have learned that the best way for our children to benefit from and succeed in school is that we—educators and parents—work together. I also know that this is easier said than done, especially with the current state of most schools and the hectic lifestyles in many of our homes. I am approaching this book the same as I approach my work: as an educational leader with a deep, courageous love and advocacy for the children and families I serve.

I am not a parent, yet I was raised by parents (three of them, in fact) and partner with parents every day. I am keenly aware and experienced about what it takes in the educational arena of parents and schools partnering to yield academic success for our children. I am using this lens and expertise to help guide parents in how to best navigate and partner with schools so that we get better results.

I know what the power of this partnership looks like and I know what it takes to foster and sustain this quality partnership. In 2002, a dear colleague and I began a thriving educational oasis intentionally designed for African-American youth in Grades 6 – 12: ASA Academy and Community Science Center ("ah-sah"). There was no achievement gap at ASA. We did our work in excellence for over seven years, sending 100% of our graduates to colleges all over the nation. We closed in 2009 due to the economic downturn and the lack of philanthropy during that time. The loss of ASA left a void for many; however, the lives that ASA touched have been forever enhanced, mine included.

It was the dream and vision of ASA that catapulted me into a deeper understanding of education and the needs of urban youth and youth of color. It is because of ASA that I was able to formulate and create educational strategies and practices that validate my beliefs of how the partnership of home and school must be tightly connected for the ultimate success of our children. It is because of ASA that I know how to identify and create powerful academic school culture that is palpable and facilitates transformational achievement. It is because of ASA that I have forged relationships with powerful dynamic "parent champions" who delay their own gratification and educate their children with the attitude of "by any means necessary."

It is because of ASA that I have developed into the educational leader I am, serving thousands under my current principalship. I am centered, focused, and knowing in the strength of my gifts and vision to do what was at the core of the initial vision: to create a model school that meets the needs of urban youth beyond test scores and close the academic and racial achievement gaps with the populations it serves.

What this book offers has been witnessed, used, developed, and supported in schools where I have taught and led. I offer first-hand guidance and experienced advice to parents who are in need of additional support to create both school success and a college-going attitude outside of school. Through strategies and tools, I will coach you into a *Parent*

Champion—so you are able to successfully champion the academic success of your child. Each chapter ends with a concrete "Next Level Action Agenda" for you to utilize as you see fit as well as writing space to capture your initial thoughts.

The *Parent Champion* is an empowerment model of support that can be implemented immediately to increase parent engagement and student success. My goal in this work is to present solid strategies, tools, and supports to empower parents to best serve their children to survive, thrive, and achieve in our educational systems.

This *Parent Champion* book will:

- Inspire you to be better partners with teachers and the school
- Empower you with tools to support your child's academic success
- Educate you on how to create a "college-going" attitude at home
- Create peace in your home from a shared set of expectations about school and clear strategies of how to reach those expectations

It is critical that we heed the teachings of the *Parent Champion*, and I encourage parents to unify to demand higher standards and results from our schools, participate more fully in the realization of those expectations, serve as contributing authors of the agendas in our schools, and take more definitive action in our homes. *Parent Champion* shares important aspects of exactly how you can do that.

We can win this race to close the achievement gap for our children. It will begin with one child at a time, your child first.

Thinking 100 years ahead on behalf of us all,
Tovi C. Scruggs
Visionary & Educational Leader
Oakland, CA - January 2014

CHAPTER ONE

What is a Parent Champion?

CHAPTER ONE

What is a Parent Champion?

Parent Champions are committed to winning school success and academic achievement for their children. Parent Champions demonstrate this commitment with appropriate actions, words, and choices regarding their children's education. When parents champion their child's school success, academic achievement becomes the priority, and the use of time and financial choices are guided by that motivation. Parent Champions focus on "educational parenting." By doing so, parents are the very best school-partners because they are *reflective and take action* in regard to how they *co-educate and partner* with their child's school in order to get the best results for their child.

As a parent, YOU are the best champion of your child's success. Being a Parent Champion means prioritizing (making the choice to give highest importance to) hands-on time and developing strategies for your child and their education. As a parent, when you prioritize time invested in education and educational choices, you are modeling your value for education and, therefore, championing your child's success and academic achievement.

Overall Message From Chapter One

As a parent, YOU are the best champion of your child's success. Being a Parent Champion means prioritizing (making the choice to give highest importance to) hands-on time and developing strategies for your child and their education. Parent Champions focus on "educational parenting."

Parent Champion Precepts:

1. Educational parenting is different than parenting, requiring me to be a true partner with my child's school to get the academic results I want to see for my child.
2. Prioritize hands-on time as it relates to educational parenting.
3. I am my child's role-model in placing value on education.

Next Level Action Agenda:

1. Keep an open-mind.
2. Be reflective about my educational parenting to date.

3. Take action to go next level—wherever that is for me—in being a Parent Champion.

Thoughts & Reflections:

CHAPTER TWO

The Critical First Step:
Reflecting on Your Parenting

CHAPTER TWO

The Critical First Step:
Reflecting on Your Parenting

As a parent, you must acknowledge the fact that you are your child's first and greatest teacher. Your child begins to learn from you both before and after birth. Your child's success depends on you. While you cannot control everything your child experiences or chooses, you can certainly influence how your child makes decisions and navigates school and life. You must embrace this truth. Once you have a child, you become a *parent*, not an easy job and not one to be taken lightly. As with all jobs that we choose, the job is done well with focus, investment, and development. The job of "parent" rarely has any preparation other than our own experience as a child, watching others, and then the nine months to strive to earn your Parenting Ph.D. before you get to work with highly intensive on-the-job-training.

As a coach, I value high levels of self-reflection and encourage others to first reflect before beginning any area of personal growth and development. Because you are reading *Parent Champion*, I trust that you are willing to look at other ways to be a better parent in the area of education—and that is commendable. Reflection and willingness to be better takes courage. As with all areas of personal growth and development, you must be willing to take an honest look at yourself and ask, "Have I been 'parenting' or have I simply been a 'parent'?" As a "parent," you are actively involved in caring for someone else, but "parent*ing*" requires deliberate action from you—a *doing* to get results.

Our greatest accountability lies in how effectively we parent. Yet, we blame the schools for the way they do what we as parents should be doing. The behaviors that our children are exhibiting are learned behaviors. We have to be honest and acknowledge that all behaviors are not learned only at school. The best way for parents to know if the moral character and behaviors being taught at home are being shown at school is to ask the child's teacher if those character traits and behaviors are being exemplified. We know that our children know how to behave and have embodied a teaching or behavior when they do it when we adults are not watching, when they do it fully on their own based on what has been instilled.

What is key in acknowledging your role in educational parenting is this: the school has its job and the home has its job. The school and the home have different jobs, yet they have similar intentions. The "job" of the school is to educate your child as it relates to academic skills. The "job" of the home is to teach, nurture, and support the child as it relates to personal skill sets for success in life. While we may believe and expect that the school's job is more than mere education, it is not realistic in this educational and societal climate as it relates to all children, particularly children of color. More to the point, you cannot expect an institution to love your child more than you do. It's up to you to do what the school will not or cannot. It's *your* child. Thankfully, the primary intention of the school and home is shared: your child achieves academic success that readies him or her for post-secondary readiness (preparation for college or the workplace).

I encourage parents to stop asking the school to do what we know is for us to be doing, for the things that we say that we are too busy to do, the things we may not even know how to do. The school has one primary role: to teach our children the academic skills to be successful in college or the workplace. There is nothing else that we can count on them to do for our children, especially when the schools often do not reflect what we may say we value. It is the job of the parent to *partner* with the school to get the child to college and to make sure that the child has been taught the various resiliency skills to stay in college and succeed. It's your child and you cannot expect anyone to love your child more than you do.

There's only one solution: it's not about *being* right—playing the blame game—it's about *doing* what's right and what works. What appears normal is not always right. As a parent who is parenting, you must stretch and challenge yourself for the courageous and consuming actions to create a success mindset and college-going culture in your home. You must become the counter-narrative in your child's life because the narrative they get from outside of your home is loud and consistent. The "narrative" is the message that is being used and fed to your child. You must always keep in mind that your child spends more waking hours with people other than you. The other people—the music, the television, the schools, the programs—they are all communicating a narrative to your child every day. It's a narrative that often must be countered (opposed) by what *you* instilled in the beginning, continue to instill, and will instill as you become more equipped and empowered.

Since we are reflecting and you are open to *Parent Champion* coaching, I ask you to ask yourself this one hard question—and answer honestly: *"How committed am I to my child's success?"*

We invest in what we are committed to. We invest our energy, our time, our talents, our money, and our resources to what we are committed to. As it relates to the success of your child in school, how committed are you to your child's success? First, what are you defining as "success" for your child? There are other barometers that are personal and individualized based on values, ethics, and morals and this guide is not the appropriate avenue for that conversation. As a school leader, the biggest factor in "success" for me as it relates to our children is that they are academically proficient, performing at or above grade level.

What kind of investment of your energy and time did you make in selecting your child's school? Did you visit first or did you let the enrollment process decide? Did the school's reputation decide? Did word of mouth decide? Did convenience decide? How many times have you gone to your child's school - more than to simply enroll, register, drop off the paperwork, and do those easy "get him in school" tasks? Some people spend more time investigating and selecting a cell phone than they do deciding what school their child will attend. How much time you spent selecting your child's school is a sign of your level of commitment to your child's success.

Did you investigate or address the reasons why your child was performing at a B or lower in a subject? Did you get a tutor when your child was struggling to do well in a class? Did you get remedial help for your child if/when you found out he was performing below grade level in reading or math? How immediate and responsive you are to being proactive about academic achievement is a sign of your level of commitment to your child's success.

Do you know what book your child is reading right now? Our children should be reading books both in and out of school, books that interest and challenge them. The library has books—thousands of them—for free. Not only does that save you money, it's also a wonderful, most memorable, and affordable way to get quality time with your child. Some of the best times spent with my mother were our trips to the library every two weeks. Not only did I become a better reader, I learned how to be resourceful and use a library, develop a love for certain authors and genres, and was able to predict quality time with my mother, leading to emotional security. From an academic perspective, the more time your child spends reading, the better he usually gets at both reading *and* writing, as he is seeing examples of proper grammar and language use that he can apply in his schoolwork.

Further, you sitting with your child while reading a book of your own for 30 minutes each day while your child also reads a book of his own is one of the most impactful examples of the importance of reading that you can provide. I know you know that children (like we all do) look to people's actions more than their words for the truth. Your level of interest in reading and the importance of reading is a sign of your level of commitment to your child's success.

If it's your biggest dream that your child do well in school and go to college, then ask yourself, "Do I want my child to achieve academic success so he or she can go to college?" If yes, the other questions are: Are you preparing your child by your actions at home and parenting in a way that supports his dreams? Are you displaying and creating a college-going attitude and home environment? Do you know enough about getting your child to college? Do you know what you don't know? Are you seeking support? The steps and investments you are taking *now* in getting your child to college are signs of your level of commitment to your child's success. It's important to mention that you can begin asking yourself these questions as early as when your child begins school. After all, once your child is school-age, your role of educational parenting begins.

A parenting investment also includes saving money if your child is going to college. Are you preparing financially? How much money have you saved? That is a sign of your level of commitment to your child's success. Let me be clear about paying for college: while all parents are not able to pay for college, this does not mean that your child should not be groomed and prepared for college as the next step. Don't limit your child by what you feel you are able to do or not do. If you know you will not be able to pay for college, your child deserves to know that; discuss it while exploring other ways to pay for college. Allow me to share: as a teen, I knew that I was paying for part of my college education; I knew I would take out loans. I am not opposed to taking out loans for college nor am I opposed to encouraging students to do the same. If I take out a $150,000 loan and I'm making near that salary each year, then who is winning? I'm winning—that is a worthwhile investment in me. That's a worthwhile investment in me making 50 times that amount over the course of my working career, a valuable investment indeed. Provide that clarity about paying for college with your child—those are good conversations to have.

What does your child want to do for a career? Do her gifts/talents even fit that career—or is she just telling you what she thinks you want to hear? The way your child plays, spends her time, and what gets her attention—all reveal to you what interests her. And whatever her passion is, her vision is—it comes from her and her spirit—so that makes it very real and worth paying attention to for signs of direction. In order for your child to be most successful, feed that vision that is coming from her instead of focusing on what you wish for your child to become. You have your own opportunity to walk in your vision for yourself; allow your child her vision for herself. How much you invest in your child's passions and talents is a sign of your level of commitment to your child's success.

As a high school educator and principal for the last 18 years, enough cannot be said about the role of parent involvement in a child's life, as it is often the best predictor of academic success and educational achievement. A key area where parents and our society miss this mark is that we think parent involvement is only valuable up to a certain point. To the contrary, parent involvement is needed for *all* 13 years of school and then for at least the first year of college. You will not get this time back so you must be actively parenting and partnering now because you will not get a "do-over." What you sow into your child now is the seed that will produce a crop and grow into the harvest. How committed are you to a large and bountiful harvest?

As part of the vision I had for school-parent partnerships at ASA Academy (the private school designed for African-American children Grades 6 –12 that I co-founded), I introduced a parent assessment tool called *Principal Kafele's 50 T's for Effective Parenting.* This particularly strong set of questions for parents can also be used as affirmations or intentions to help focus your parenting and identify areas where you may have gaps you need to close, as well as acknowledge areas where you are excelling. At ASA, we even took it a step further and created the same list for students to assess what they felt they were learning from their parents as it related to the list—this helps you to identify if your narrative is being heard. I invite you to do the same with your child when you are ready for that type of delving into your educational parenting as it relates to your child.

Graciously, Principal Baruti Kafele gave me permission to use and publish the list. (While Principal Kafele designed it for African-American parents, I have used it successfully with other demographic groups; to do this, just make needed substitutions in the questions and terminology as appropriate. To keep the integrity of Principal Kafele's intellectual property, I do not modify his wording). I am deeply grateful to him and his permission speaks to the unity, shared gifts, and teamwork that need to be more intentional for the betterment and success of our youth. The list is also published in his book, *A Black Parent's Handbook to Educating Your Children (Outside of the Classroom)*, which I highly recommend.

Please write a "yes" OR "no" OR "maybe" next to each statement.

1. I am a parent to my children.

2. I am my children's first teacher.

3. I require my children to read books and newspapers daily.

4. I require my children to write early.

5. I read to my children.

6. I require that my children read African-centered literature towards their life long study of their history.

7. I educate myself in order to educate my children about their history.

8. I teach my children about the struggle and their roles in the struggle.

9. I talk to my children about having pride in who and what they are.

10. I conduct myself as a role model for my children—I lead by example.

11. I remind my children that they represent me at all times.

12. I spend quality time with my children.

13. I communicate with my children regularly—both speaking and listening.

14. I have high expectations for my children, despite my own setbacks.

15. I constantly encourage my children to search for the genius and creativity that lies within them.

16. I constantly challenge my children to achieve academic excellence.

17. I hold my children accountable for achieving academic excellence.

18. I strive to motivate, educate, and empower my children daily.

19. I do not accept mediocrity from my children.

20. I tell and show my children that I love them.

21. I don't ridicule and demean my children.

22. I refrain from negativity in my interactions with my children.

23. I take my children to African-centered educational programs and activities.

24. I expose my children to a wide variety of activities.

25. I assist my children with their homework.

26. I review my children's homework.

27. I require that my children study—even when they do not have homework.

28. I attend functions and meetings at my children's school.

29. I go to my children's school to meet and interact with teachers and administrators.

30. I encourage my children to believe in themselves.

31. I assist my children with determining a purpose in life.

32. I assist my children with understanding that they have a historical obligation to achieve.

33. I encourage my children to be determined to desire success from within.

34. I encourage my children to develop a vision for success.

35. I require that my children are goal-oriented.

36. I talk to my children about societal issues and problems as they relate to individual and community empowerment.

37. I talk to my children about expected and acceptable behavior both in and out of school.

38. I discipline my children appropriately.

39. I teach my children positive values.

40. I teach my children about household responsibilities.

41. I teach my children conflict resolution.

42. I teach my children coping and survival skills.

43. I monitor my children's media exposure.

44. I monitor who my children spend their time with.

45. I provide for my children while not depriving them of their needs.

46. I teach my children about good hygiene and grooming.

47. I monitor my children's attire and overall appearance and have a say in what they wear and how they wear it.

48. I talk to my children about respecting adults.

49. I talk to my children about proper relations with the opposite gender.

50. I talk to my son about respecting, valuing, appreciating, and getting along with other Black men.

For some parents, the above statements are difficult and challenging on several levels. That's okay; you are taking the time to reflect and empower yourself and that takes courage—the key quality that champions are made of. In order for your child to succeed in school and life, you must get in touch with your expectations and act/make choices accordingly. You are holding *The Parent Champion* with the intention of meeting the responsibility you have been given as a parent; be gentle with yourself, commend your willingness and take action where you are clear.

Overall Message From Chapter Two

Reflection and willingness to be better takes courage. As with all areas of personal growth and development, you must be willing to take an honest look at yourself and decide where you are going to improve. Know your job as parent as it pertains to *educational parenting.*

Parent Champion Precepts:

1. The home and school have different roles and jobs to fulfill in the life of my child. It is important not to try to make them the same.

2. I invest my time, resources, focus, and energy in what I am committed to.

3. My narrative with my child must be stronger than the narrative he hears outside of my home.

4. Don't wait or lose time. I must be proactive about my child's academic achievement.

Next Level Action Agenda:

1. Read with my child daily, even if it's only 20 minutes.

2. Talk to my child about college and future plans and goals.

3. Take Principal Kafeli's "50 I's for Effective Parenting" survey and reflect upon my answers.

4. Identify my narrative and discover if it is being heard.

Thoughts & Reflections:

CHAPTER THREE

Vision is the Physician

CHAPTER THREE

Vision is the Physician

Every person holds a vision for how they choose to be in the world. I believe that your vision is communicated to you from your inner-self, and when we are tapped in to our spirit, we are able to see our vision and how to live and walk in that vision more freely. Your vision can be whatever you choose; some people have grandiose visions and some people have more simple visions. Either is absolutely fine. Whatever your vision, you are here to live it, to make it manifest.

"Vision" sounds very fancy but it's really a mode of seeing or conceiving what is pictured in the mind or senses; the power of imagination to see what you want your reality to be. That's what a vision is. It is important not to confuse a "vision" with "visualization," as they are two different things. Vision is like a "snap-shot" you may get about your future that just appears in your mind, even from a daydream. Vision comes through the open-mind of a receptive space of allowing for an image to come. The exact opposite is "visualization" which is useful forced imagery in your mind to make something happen. Once you see aspects or parts of your vision in your mind, then it is important to step back and ask, "What are the steps and goals that I need to do to achieve that vision? Am I in alignment with my actions to achieve that vision?"

Just as it's important that you have a vision for your own life, it's important that you also have a vision for your role as a parent and for your family. As a leader in the home, the Parent Champion has a vision for his family. Your vision for your family will help to keep you focused on investing your time, resources, and energy on what you say is important for you and your family, much of which will include your child's academic success.

A vision is different from your mission. Your mission is *why* you do something, but your vision is *how* it looks to be living —expressing—your mission. For example, my personal mission statement is to "inspire, educate, and empower people of all ages to create their best lives." My vision for how I live my mission is that I use my life examples and stories to inspire others, I educate both teens and adults, I lead workshops and coach on personal and professional growth, and I have now authored the very book you are reading. These are various ways that I continue to express my mission and it keeps me focused - aligned - on making choices and taking action that help me to accomplish my goals and dreams. You, too, can do this.

Have you ever written the vision you see for yourself? For your family? For your parenting? For clarity in how you choose to move forward in making decisions for yourself, your home, and your child, it's imperative that you to take the time get clear on your vision. If you don't know your vision, sit and have a good conversation with yourself, and maybe even with God. Sit and get clear about your family lifestyle to achieve a culture of success or college-going culture. Ask questions: What must I embrace to achieve the vision? What must I release? What gifts do I already bring? What kind of support do I need to bring the vision alive? Some of these questions come from a very powerful process designed by Michael

Beckwith called "visioning." If you are not familiar with it, I have offered it as a key resource at the end of the guide.

Visioning is a process that allows for the exposure and unfolding of purpose and clarity; I have used it for myself, with students, with families, and with clients with great success. At ASA, we would hold visioning circles, allowing for the children to connect to their inner selves. They would answer the above questions and then we would have explicit conversations and planning guides to connect their school success to their vision, which resulted in greater focus on academics because they could see the direct link of their academic actions to school success to the vision that they hold for their lives.

Again, your child has a vision too. Your job as a parent is to equip your child to live his vision, not create or choose his vision for him. I can not emphasize this enough. For her to be truly successful, support your child in identifying her vision, nurture her vision, and allow her vision to be the blue-print to guide academic choices and next steps. Her vision

44

can serve as a reminder of staying focused and aligning choices.

Your vision as it relates to parenting should focus with the end in mind. Parenting not only for school, but for beyond school, parenting for how your child takes what you instilled in him to live his life.

Overall Message From Chapter Three

Your vision for your family will help to keep you focused on investing your time, resources, and energy on what you say is important for you and your family, much of which will include your child's academic success.

Parent Champion Precepts:

1. Having a vision is important, for both my child and for me.

2. I have a vision and my child does too. I do not force my vision for my child on him, allowing him to have his own vision.

3. Visioning is a process that allows for the exposure and unfolding of purpose and clarity.

Next Level Action Agenda:

1. Develop my vision for my family.

2. Identify and articulate clear action steps for my family to live out the vision.

3. Support my child in identifying his own vision.

Thoughts & Reflections:

CHAPTER FOUR

*Concrete Strategies, Actions, Tasks,
and Tools for Parent Champions*

CHAPTER FOUR

Concrete Strategies, Actions, Tasks, and Tools for Parent Champions

After reflection and vision building, it's time to take action where you are clear. While you may not be ready to do it all or not need to do it all, you are always at a place where you can make one type of change—large or small—that will create a new trajectory in a direction that better serves you and your family. Changing one dynamic can change an outcome.

A key aspect of educational parenting is in your home. Your home is a place of preparation. Parent Champions not only prepare their children for life; they also prepare them for where they spend most of their time: at school. Because of this, your home—whether it's a studio apartment or a mini-mansion—is a place where your child learns *your* academic expectations for his success. I can not stress enough how your expectations of your child's performance at school must be created in your home first – through your vision, your narrative, and your actions. Remember, your vision sets the tone for your child's personal vision and your narrative must be louder than the other narratives your child is exposed to. You must also limit his exposure to other visions and narratives. This is best done by structured action: enforce daily study time with limited television and Internet time.

Limited Television and/or Screen-time

While teaching at ASA, we learned that a non-ASA family had a rule in their home: no television Monday–Thursday. Prior to creating this rule, this scholarly family was struggling with focusing their very smart children on school so they could produce quality work. They knew they had to do something impactful to show their children what they meant about the importance of school so they instituted this house rule—for everyone. This also meant that they had to up their parenting game (refer to "50 I's for Effective Parenting" #10).

Our children have to understand that we are preparing them for *their* lives, not watching other's visions through the "tella-lie-vision." When the child knows there is no TV to watch, they stop rushing to get work half-done; they stop rushing to be less-than organized; they stop rushing to study less; they stop rushing through the reading assignment, they stop rushing to rush...all because they are not rushing to the scheduled TV show. They will see they are on your schedule—the schedule of excelling in school and preparing for success after high school. TV will become less important. The DVR is great if you have that to record shows to watch later. TV is a privilege to be earned after the primary job of schoolwork is done.

When we instituted this request to ASA Families, other unexpected results occurred too. Families reported an increase in peace in their homes, greater quality family time (they were not in different rooms watching different things), and, of course, we were all able to report an increase in the quality of academic work and attitude that was really the central goal of the policy's implementation.

As you take control of the peace and schedule of your home, I cannot suggest strongly enough that you confiscate cell phones (and any other mobile electronics) every night. Our children are not sleeping because they are using social media or texting or talking well into the early morning. They have told me this themselves and we see the evidence—fatigue, low achievement, and a bad attitude/mood due to exhaustion. We must help children to help themselves, by taking those cell phones and electronics every weeknight. I think we can all agree that no one is calling your child in the middle of the night for an emergency that a child or teen truly has the capacity or resources to solve.

This aspect of your parenting may feel difficult, as your children may initially rebuke this…and maybe even sneak into your room looking for their phone. It is up to us—the adults—to remind the children who is in charge: you are. You are the leader in your home. A Parent Champion is not parenting to please to their children, but to raise their children and empower them for greatness.

Be Proactive

One of the most important things that you can do as a Parent Champion is to be proactive versus reactive. In my career, so many parents have come to me when the child is already behind three to four years in reading. That means the problem been going on three to four years! From the very moment that you find out that there is a deficit in achievement or development or skill building, you must take action. You must be proactive instead of reactive, because waiting to correct a problem could result in it being too late.

Taking action often means doing something extra, but most important, doing something that has not yet been done. If you do only more of what has already been done, then you may not get a better result. For instance, if your child is not doing well in math and you find this out six weeks into the school year, then that is the time that you increase study time AND get a tutor. Each year of school builds on the next; that's why children can get "years behind" in learning, we let the problem go on too long believing (or hoping) that it will remedy itself, change later in the school year, or simply get better with a new teacher a year later. This is all too often *not* the case.

From personal experience as a student, I have fond memories of being miserable with my college-student Algebra tutor after school. The reason I can look back "fondly" is because I know my mother acted like a Parent Champion—she got me a tutor immediately when she saw that my struggle was more than what could be remedied by the teacher; it was obvious I needed more time and attention to gain those concepts. Some say tutors are too expensive, however I didn't keep my tutor for the whole year; my tutor was utilized only when I needed help filling in gaps in my understanding. We were not wealthy and my mother had to stretch her resources to make my tutoring strategic and pay off. These days, most schools and public libraries have free after-school tutoring programs. Be proactive: ask.

I also saw this same type of Parent Champion behavior by a 4.0 student at ASA. As talented and scholarly as this student was, she struggled to grow as a writer in my English class. She had the basics and general concepts, but her challenges came with extrapolation and voice. For some reason, I could not reach her to promote those areas of growth. Her mother got a writing tutor who focused on those areas. Taking this initiative created change within weeks, and the improvement was obvious and worth the investment of time and money.

Part of the beauty in that situation was that the mother (much like my own) did not criticize the teacher (me!) or complain that I was not reaching her daughter in this specific area; she acknowledged how much her child was learning yet also acknowledged that there are times when *another* teacher-voice is needed. There are times when we need to hear the same thing differently because we learn differently. This is partially why extra help from the core teacher may not always yield results; there are times when you need a different style, different strategy, and different voice.

In summary, the key point is to take action where you are clear if additional action is needed; do not waste time. Be proactive.

School Visits &
The Family School Partnership Act

There are important considerations you should make before selecting or visiting your child's school. When you go to visit the school, it's critical that you stay a few hours, especially at lunchtime. That's when what's really real is front and center because everyone's guard is down. What do you hear in the hallways? How are children engaging with each other? How is staff spending class time and out-of-class time? How is the staff morale/energy/attitude? What is your child learning? What strategies are the teachers using? Simply lecture? Other activities? How does your child learn best—and are those techniques being utilized?

If you are visiting to select a new school for your child, then you want to be sure to go to the classes of his *next* grade level because you want to make sure that the class is doing new things, not what your child is already doing. After all, remediation is not the responsibility of the school; the school should be teaching what the standards articulate and moving forward each month and each year. If the same school is doing another year of teaching and remediating at the next grade level, then the school is not producing its own scholars at grade level, which is not a good sign.

Interestingly enough, our own government acknowledges that we have to be proactive instead of reactive, hence Labor Code 230.8, which is the Family School Partnership Act. I continue to be astounded as to why this act is not widely publicized and articulated in every school newsletter, website, and bulletin board. The Family School Partnership Act allows parents to take off from work for school-related business for their child, up to 40 hours per year. I have often written letters to parents' employers citing this act so that they may be more engaged; any good school would enthusiastically provide such a letter to you if necessary. Often the first thing that comes to mind for why parents might use this time is because you have to get your child out of trouble. That would be reaction and not pro-action. Further, that under-utilizes this law, which is *not* an act of a Parent Champion. Use this 40 hours to attend school events, volunteer, chaperone a trip, meet with teachers, or simply to visit the school at your convenience to observe your child's world at school more fully. It is time well spent. This law serves you to serve your child by freeing you to partner with the school.

It bears mentioning that the older your child gets, the more she will not want you at her school. You being at her school does not always mean that you have to be her shadow or for her to even know you are there. You are the parent and how you choose to spend your time in educational parenting is your business and your responsibility, not the child's. Again, you are the leader of your family, and you know that your educational parenting actions will result in better academic achievement for your child. That is the focus and the goal of educational parenting and you cannot meet that goal without being at school frequently and regularly.

Meditation

From my own 20 years of daily conscious meditation time, I deem it a critical requirement to unlocking some of our best thinking. Plus, it's a wonderful way to bring peace to your home, spend quality time with your child, and create higher levels of achievement for you both. There are creative insights, ideas, and solutions waiting to be given to you and your child, but we have to stop and allow for a deeper listening from our inner-self.

Academic achievement, greatness, and genius require a level of fostered creative intelligence. Creative intelligence requires quiet time. This is often underestimated and not discussed in our society as a way to *be* smart. The quiet time that fosters creative intelligence is often referred to as meditation or mindfulness. For my own daily quiet meditation practice and what I teach to others of all ages is this: sit comfortably and quietly with your eyes closed and simply breathe. Allow your body and mind to become still as thoughts simply flow in and out. Just focus on your rhythmic breathing, in and out, with repetition. It's a daily practice and, trust me, it's called a *practice* for a reason; it's meant to be done regularly and consistently like anything else you want to get better at and embody with ease. Even after 20 years of meditating, there are still some days when I feel as though I cannot still my thoughts from racing or I would rather skip doing it altogether—but I don't allow that resistance to stop me. I have come to experience and realize the fact that the benefits far outweigh some of the challenges. Each experience of meditation is generally different each and every time, and the more we do it, the easier it becomes.

Because meditation/mindfulness is becoming more popular and mainstream, numerous studies have been published about the positive results (increased academic performance, increased emotional intelligence/conflict control, reduced stress, reduced depression and anxiety, reduced symptoms of ADD/ADHD, reduced blood pressure in at-risk teens, and reduced use of medications—if you want to learn more or verify, I encourage you to search the Internet). In fact, there are several programs facilitating mediation in schools throughout the country. The good news is that it's easy and it's free. So, whether or not your child's school has a program, you can facilitate this at home.

At ASA, I taught students as young as 6th grade to sit for 20 minutes every morning without interruption. As a school of 6th–12th grade students and teachers (some parents would often stay and join us too), we would "sit" each morning to get focused and ready for our day of learning as a community. There were kids who would say, "That changed the way I lived day to day." We could see, and they would sometimes admit, if they didn't meditate, their day was off-balance.

As a result of their positive experience with meditation at school, parents began to have their children meditate on weekends because it changed the energy and climate of their homes. And you can do it *with* your child—it's quality time. It's simply an act of creating peace and clarity. Further, meditation has been proven to reduce stress and anxiety. It's safe to say that the majority of our children—be it a by-product of school and/or home—are stressed, having at least some level of anxiety. It is challenging to focus on learning and school when stressed or anxious.

It's important to note that even our students diagnosed with ADD/ADHD were able to sit and meditate, and we all reported an increase in the positive behavior and focus during class as a result of meditation.

Meditation is a tool for academic success that begins in the homes of Parent Champions.

In Conclusion

To conclude this chapter, we must recognize that there is a foundation of action that must be laid as part of educational parenting. While there is much to do, it is not about doing more of the same to get the same results. We have to do things differently, and we have to do better. My father says, "You've got to be ready so you don't have to get ready." Preparation is always more time consuming than the actual doing for what you have prepared. Historically, many families, particularly those of color, have lived in poor and impoverished situations and were still able to achieve above-standard results. Today, we have an abundance of resources and above-standard "everything" yet we are yielding grossly sub-standard results. Achievement is not an issue of wealth; it's an issue of a parent's commitment to the success of their child. A deep showing of that commitment is taking action. We cannot turn our children over to institutions to do the work that is *our* work to do. We have to do better. We must focus on educational parenting in addition to parenting.

Overall Message From Chapter Four

While you may not be ready to do it all or not need to do it all, you are always at a place where you can make one type of change – large or small – that will create a new trajectory in a direction that better serves you and your family. Changing one dynamic can change an outcome.

Parent Champion Precepts:

1. Take action where I am clear, even if I am nervous or fearful.

2. My home is a place of preparation.

3. As the parent, I am in charge.

Next Level Action Agenda:

1. Limit screen-time.

2. Confiscate technology before bedtime.

3. Be proactive about achievement.

4. Visit my child's school.

5. Begin or resume a meditation practice with my child.

Thoughts & Reflections:

CHAPTER FIVE

Effective School Partnering: Building the Bridge of the Home and School Connection

CHAPTER FIVE

Effective School Partnering: Building the Bridge of the Home and School Connection

A successful parent-educator relationship models for the child that an entire team of adults is on his side and working to co-create his greatness and genius.

When parents and educators work well together and share the common goal of fully developing a child, everyone benefits. This working relationship does *not* outgrow you or your child; it is expected to last until your child graduates from high school.

From the age a child enters school until she leaves school, her two most paramount and time-consuming "worlds" are those of home and school. As a child ages, she will spend more time in her academic world than she will in her home world. It is crucial that a positive relationship exists between the two worlds, as they should not operate in a void, one separate from the other. The spiritual principle *"there is no separation"* comes to my mind as a concept for visualizing the home and school connection for the success of our youth. Again, we are in a partnering relationship of "we, us, and ours" as it relates to the education and success of our children. We are in this together and our children need us to be fully engaged in this together.

Further, parents and educators can provide each other with unique insights and different perspectives about the same child, culminating in a more complete understanding of that child's abilities, strengths, and challenges. The educator knows more about curriculum and the school culture, while parents know more about the child's personality, tendencies, patterns, and family life. Further, as a child grows and matures, an educator can provide valuable insight into how she is developing a personal work ethic, work habits, and working relationships that may often look different than those displayed at home.

To launch the home and school connection in a positive way, the attitude a parent displays about school is crucial. This goes far beyond the "you need to do well in school" speech that parents often deliver. Because young children, in particular, identify strongly with their parents, the display of attitudes, values, and innermost feelings are contagious. They become embedded in the child's mind at the deepest levels. In my experience as an educator, I have found many children's views about education, success in school, and respecting adults is often influenced by both the verbal and non-verbal expressions and feelings of the parent—you.

If your experience with school was miserable, you might feel anxious about your child's school experiences. Your child will sense this, and it could impair her ability to throw herself wholeheartedly into learning. Further, for the child's sake, you need to put the past in the past and "start over"—assuming that your child's teachers, school, and overall experience will be positive. Even if you didn't like school, the best way to help your child is to endorse his experience: get involved, be positive, and trust his teachers. He will get the message: "School is important; I want you to engage fully." In addition, it is imperative that you do not speak negatively to a teacher or about a teacher in the presence of your child. This is often irreversibly damaging to the relationship between your child and the teacher, as the student often then feels free to disregard and/or disrespect the teacher, often not working to his highest level because you have modeled that the teacher can be disregarded or disrespected. The student actually becomes less engaged in the teacher's class. Less attitudinal engagement often results in less academic engagement—doing less work. The end result? Your child's achievement and school record suffers. For some reason in a child's mind, that loss of regard correlates to a loss of effort towards academic achievement in that teacher's class. Again, as the parent, you are your child's example of valuing education and those that educate him.

After the right attitude and outlook has been set, it is important to address the "nuts and bolts" of the home and school connection. In addition to the full-time job that many parents have outside of the home, parents must look at educating their youth as their *second* full-time job. A parent does not have to take on the role of educator; however, it is crucial that the parent see his role as *facilitating and overseeing* the education of the child as a full-time job. It's both a responsibility and a necessity. Generally, youth do not have the discipline, experience, or skill-sets to facilitate their success in school without the guidance of a parent at home and a caring educator at school. Remember, *"There is no separation."*

Below are some tasks, action-items, and skill-sets to help ensure the home-school connection so that your children do well in school. They are closely linked and build upon each other. Remember, changing a dynamic can change an outcome.

1. **<u>Have High Expectations</u>:** Let youth know that they don't have to be the best as long as they are *doing* their best. Set a high bar and put supports in place to reach that bar. Reward solid efforts as well as achievements. Look for growth, not perfection, praising the effort more than the outcome. Excellence only comes with the growth that practice brings (and practice takes time). In fact, there is a powerful book by Carol Dweck titled *Mindset: The New Psychology of Success* that discusses the

power of praising our children's effort growth process rather than the simple outcome. Instilling a sense of pride in my work as a child, my mother would make me recopy my work until it was neat and then it got to the point where I would demand that of myself and take that level of care. Unless we get to that point where we are demanding a level of care and having high expectations for our children, the child doesn't really know to even do that for herself. Often the expectations are not as high from teachers. The expectations of the classroom should not be higher than the expectations set at home for your child. That level of pride, excellence, resilience, and quality will take your child far no matter whose classroom they are in.

2. **Use Routines:** As adults, we govern and design our own routines. Work your child's routine into your own for the ease of time, learning, and spending time together. Make lunches together, get clothes ready for the next

day together, read together, gather the next day's materials by the door together. By establishing routines together, a parent is also teaching his child or teen how to establish and follow his own routines that support successful habits of mind and action that, in turn, supports school success.

3. **Organization:** Organization is a weak area for many children and parents, but a serious key to success. Routines, structure, and organization all work together to create a sense of peace and accomplishment. Organization also sets the stage for success in the other areas of "doing school." Your organizational systems will look different based on your family dynamics; but no matter what your family dynamic is, I have two "best tips" that will improve your level of organization immediately:

   - TIP #1—A Calendar—plot out <u>every</u> school date that relates to your child on your personal calendar and post a large wall-calendar (showing all 12 months) in a central area of your home (back of a door, side of the refrigerator, hallway wall, etc.). You can not be in two places at once; having your child's school events on your work/personal calendar will ensure your availability to attend the school events. Academic school events are priority over work and socializing. Remember, you cannot get that time back for your child's school, but your work will always be there, especially by utilizing the Family Partnership Act.

- TIP #2: Purchase a six-shelf sweater organizer and hang it in a convenient closet. Label each shelf with the day of the week and place your child's items for each day in the proper slot. For example, if you have soccer practice on Wednesday, then shin-guards, cleats, and uniform would go in the Wednesday slot. This can be done each week as a family ritual on Sundays to prepare for the week, and maintained each night as you prepare for the next morning. I recommend that each child have their own organizer, and I recommend using it in the child's room or in a closet near the front door (or wherever you gather your items for each day). Your mornings will be much easier (and sane) with this system, and it creates autonomy for your child.

4. **<u>Meet and Greet:</u>** Plan a time to sit and discuss your child with her teachers. Discuss areas of success, improvement, and growth-goals. This is best done three to four times each year. A concerned, responsible educator would never avoid meeting or communicating with a parent. This is also a time to clearly express to teachers your expectations (from #1 above) and plans for your child, as well as how you can work together in holding your child accountable to ensure those expectations are met. And if you tell the teacher you are going to do something, be sure to follow through. You want them to

take you seriously. Express that you are there to create a win-win partnership for your child's success. Make it clear: you see yourself as a team and you value the teachers' efforts with your child.

5. **<u>Support the School:</u>** Parents should attend school meetings, join the PTSA or similar organization to have your voice heard and get support from other parents, volunteer at least three times each school year, and remember to act from a standpoint of *educational parenting* (see Chapter 1). This shows youth that parents are connected to educators and the education process. This shows youth that everyone cares and *"there is no separation."* Again, be sure to start off the school year by getting a school calendar of dates, and then placing those dates on to your own personal calendar. There is no excuse for accidentally double-booking yourself or being caught by surprise with a school event that has been on your personal calendar since August.

6. **READ!**: Youth must read in every subject that they study. Please support good reading habits by modeling literacy (going to the library and reading for recreation). It's best to make sure that your child is reading at least one book outside of his school books. Reading is like any other skill – you get better at it the more you do it. Further, parents can ask teachers for good general comprehension questions to ask about your child's reading. You can do this in the car or in line at the store: ask your child to tell you about the information he's reading. Dig deep by asking character names, details, setting, character relationships, etc. Make him *think* about what he is reading, not just recount the plot or details. This will improve verbal expression, articulation of ideas, and reading comprehension skills. It helps to train your child to look at reading as a means to gain understanding. These interactions also show that you value his knowledge and opinion, building your own relationship and connection.

7. **Monitor Schoolwork/Homework:** Offer to help, but do not do the work. Look through the youth's notebook/folder at least once each week to monitor progress, feedback, and assignments. You definitely want to use what we affectionately termed at ASA the "Let Me See It Policy." When your child tells you her homework is completed, you want to respond, "Let me see it." This keeps your child accountable and you will be aware of the quality of work she is producing.

8. **Be Connected:** Having school-based conversations are part of an academic vision and preparing your child for academic success. Talking about the school day with youth shows that you care. Ask your child *real* questions about school. "How was school today?" can often be felt as generic; an authentically connected parent asks more specific questions: "Share two good things that happened during the day;" "Tell me about math class today;" "Who did you laugh with today?" "Who is

your favorite character in the book you are reading?" Have fun thinking of a creative question you can talk ask your child about school. If they cannot tell you good information—*more than surface level* answers, they are either not engaged or not learning. One or both of these things is at work and neither is acceptable for your child's education. If having these types of conversations with your child is new, be patient with both yourself and him, as they may not want to talk because it feels new. Admittedly, listening—really listening without distraction—to some of your child's stories or daily happenings can often stretch your patience, especially when it doesn't sound important. However, it's critical that you establish this listening connection now because as your child grows and matures, she will hopefully continue to share with you, trusting that you are truly listening. Stay the course, keep asking, and keep listening.

9. **Create a "Super Study Area":** This is my favorite recommendation to parents who want to bridge the home and school connection, a concept not my own but learned from the book, *Full Esteem Ahead: 100 Ways to Build Self-Esteem in Children and Adults.* A "Super Study Area" will help a youth learn how to study and take homework time more seriously. This is something that really works, costs only a little bit of money, and can ensure a more academic mindset for years to come. Creating a "Super Study Area" can be done in a corner of any room in your living space (but avoid areas of distraction and family traffic). Based on the work of Diane and Julia Loomans in *Full Esteem Ahead*, I provided the following list to parents upon enrolling their youth at ASA Academy for setting up a "Super Study Area:"

   a. Provide your youth with a good desk and comfortable chair. Second hand shopping or asking for donated items works well for this.

b. Make sure there is plenty of light in the room. Besides ceiling light, consider additional light such as a desk lamp.

c. Use a file box or small 2 drawer cabinet to provide your youth with places to file letters, papers, projects, special documents, pictures, awards, etc.

d. Provide some shelves, stacking baskets, or crates for books and materials. Be sure there is a dictionary and thesaurus.

e. Stock the desk in an organized and useful way. Stock with supplies such as paper (lined & blank), pencils, pens, erasers, scissors, glue, tape, a calculator, and a hole-punch.

f. Provide a special calendar that notes homework, projects, and special events to be posted above the desk area.

g. If it's within your budget, provide a computer and printer in your home. I don't recommend having it at the youth's desk unless he is disciplined not to "surf/play" on the computer when he should be doing other assignments. Plus, a computer is best kept in an easily monitored area.

The "Super Study Area" really supports a youth's success because it conveys the importance of school and the structure to achieve from home. In addition, it is important to cement the homework routine effectively with set hours each night that will be spent in the "Super Study Area."

When a healthy relationship exists between home and school, parents and educators value the expertise that each of them brings to the compelling life-work of educating youth. When parents and educators work together to build the foundation of home and school as a team, everyone wins. Build the bridge of home and school with awareness, caring, discipline, structure, and love because *"There is no separation."*

Overall Message From Chapter Five

Educational parenting lasts the *entire* time your child is in school. There is no separation between the home and the school.

Parent Champion Precepts:

1. I am in a partnering relationship as it relates to my child's school.

2. I have ownership over creating the home-school connection because I am the parent.

3. My child spends more time at school than at home each year.

4. Exchanging information with my child's teachers means we each get to know the whole child, not just what she shows us.

Next Level Action Agenda:

1. I need to be sure to meet and greet my child's teachers.

2. Create routines with my child at home that support academic success.

3. Get organized – at least with my calendar and night time preparation for the next day.

4. Make a "Super Study Area."

Thoughts & Reflections:

CHAPTER SIX

The Top 5 Parent Champion Behaviors

CHAPTER SIX

The Top 5 Parent Champion Behaviors

As a school leader who works with parents and students every day, I want to share with you the Top 5 Parent Champion Behaviors that are critical to true educational parenting in action. While much was offered in this book, living these 5 behaviors are fundamentally necessary as you partner with your child's school.

1. **Commit to being informed and involved.**

   What this may look like: Putting school events and dates on your calendar; joining and attending PTA/PTSA meetings or other types of councils where parent voice is invited and heard (even if you are not an officer of the council, the meetings are open), attending all academic events like Back to School Night, Report Card Nights, Open House, and parent-teacher conferences; attending two-four non-academic events (like sports or plays regardless of your child's involvement because you are both part of a school community of "we" and "us"); learning who the key people are for you and your child (the counselor, the principal, the assistant principal, the teachers); reading the school handbooks, newsletters, emails, and website; listening to the automated phone messages; and responding to emails. *NOTE* – if your child's school has a web-based communication program for parent engagement, it is critical to step #1–3 that you register and stay informed via that means of communication.

2. **Learn and understand how your child's school works.**

    What this may look like: Learning who the key people are for you and your child (the counselor, the principal, the assistant principal, the teachers); visiting the school offices to connect a name with a face; educating yourself about the school's protocols; reading the school handbooks and newsletters; putting the Attendance Office phone number in your cell phone for easy access; putting other important phone numbers in your cell phone for easy access; understanding what school councils do on your behalf; and listening to the automated phone messages.

3. **Learn and know what grades, scores, and credits your child needs to move forward from year to year, especially to graduate and be college-going.**

    What this may look like: Requesting this criteria; reading the school handbook; meeting with your child's teacher and/or counselor; closely monitoring progress at grading periods and in between; attending academic school events; and requesting a transcript every semester.

4. **Support your child's academic behavior with time, structure, and environment.**

    What this may look like: Knowing your child's learning style (see Appendix) and communicate and nurture him in this way as best you can; have a clear time and space for homework each weeknight; take time to get organized each week (includes emptying the backpack); daily use of the "let me see it" strategy; invest in a tutor when necessary; you and your child consistently reading a pleasure-reading book; and collect cell phones and other mobile electronics each school-night before bedtime.

5. **Establish a collaborative plan with your child for her future (it is never too early to do this).**

   What this may look like: Identify your child's goals and vision for herself; explore together the educational path and actions that are necessary to achieve the goals and vision; share and discuss this plan with your child's teachers and counselor; reading books, biographies, and/or magazines that align with your child's goals and vision; identify and/or research school and community programs that can nurture your child's goals and vision (after school programs, school programs, community/teen centers, and summer camps); revisit and update or modify the plan every grading period (this helps to make the connection of school success to life success— "are we on-track or off-track?").

Overall Message From Chapter Six

There are 5 key behaviors that make educational parenting most effective and there are several actions to choose from to be a better school partner in those 5 areas.

Parent Champion Precepts:

1. There are foundational behaviors to successful educational parenting and school partnering.

2. This is a major commitment to your child's academic success.

3. I know I should, and I just have to prepare myself to really do it.

Next Level Action Agenda:

1. Educate myself about school protocols.

2. Become part of the school community and be involved in PTA/PTSA.

3. Create a written plan for my child's future that we write together.

Initial Thoughts & Reflections:

CHAPTER SEVEN

Time & Space

CHAPTER SEVEN
Time & Space

I realize that some of what is written in this book may be a lot to take in, perhaps causing you to feel overwhelmed as it relates to time. There are some things I want to highlight regarding educational parenting and time.

First, educational parenting requires a shift in your mindset and your lifestyle. For your mindset, it is imperative that you see yourself as a leader of your home and of your family. As a leader, you must put into action first what you want to see from your children. You go first, and, as a result, your children will follow. It's a synergy that will get created in your home by the initial shift of you, the leader.

Second, I assert that our lifestyle (the way we live and conduct our lives) reflects what we value and deem as important. What we value and deem as important, if aligned, is where we choose to place our time and attention. Some of the time-wasters that our society has come to value as normal do not support a family lifestyle focused on academic success.

Our society continues to distract and divert our attention with busy-ness like television watching, excessive technology use, social media, and other timewasters. All of this takes away from time to do what really matters: attention to our priorities, quality time with family, quiet time for reflection, self-care, reading, and creative projects and hobbies that nurture our spirits.

With our society's culture of busyness, it may appear that you do not have a lot of time. In fact, I believe that our society is creating in us all an unhealthy psychosis as it relates to time. Being very busy at all times does not necessarily equate to achievement and/or success. It takes time to create, allow for a process, be patient, and even do nothing. We need to learn the value of using time to our advantage and realizing that we simply cannot get everything done with quality and care if we are overextended. It is time to slow down and allow for spaciousness by creating the space by focusing on what is most important: our time with our children.

Spaciousness allows for the void, an emptiness that allows for new creation. We have power in that. We have the power to fill the void with what *does* serve our families, fill the void with what *does not* serve our families, or maintain a level of spaciousness in the void to simply allow for even greater spaciousness to be more responsive as life presents itself. Just know and be mindful that the time and space will be filled with something, consciously or not.

So, the purpose here is to reassess the ways in which you are spending your time and begin to adjust what can be done differently to be more efficient, productive, and sane. While that's easier said than done, the best suggestion I can offer as a starting place is to take the strategy from Chapter 4 that was offered: cut out television Mondays – Thursdays nights. I ask you to do this for two weeks and evaluate how it has impacted your lifestyle for your family as far as creating more time, spaciousness, and peace in your home.

Educational parenting takes time and space to make your children's academic success a priority. Be honest with yourself – it's not *all* important so prioritize what is and drop what is not.

Overall Message From Chapter Seven

Educational parenting requires a shift in your mindset and your lifestyle.

Parent Champion Precepts:

1. A mindset of busy-ness is not healthy.

2. Educational parenting requires time.

3. The way I spend my time reflects my priorities.

Next Level Action Agenda:

1. Reduce and/or cut out TV.

2. Evaluate my time on social media.

3. Assess what I am making time for and what I am not making time for. Is my time spent aligned with what I say is important?

Thoughts & Reflections:

CHAPTER EIGHT

*One Last Important Note:
Trust the Process*

CHAPTER EIGHT

One Last Important Note: Trust the Process

It would not be responsible of me to offer all of this to you without being sure to include a few words of advice and caution: putting this information into your hands and empowering parents on this level is going to rock the operations of our schools and shift the status quo, causing those who lead and work in our schools to be more mindful of bringing parents back into the equation of our service more intentionally and meaningfully. As I stated before, the schools are not serving you fully. Schools and school leaders will need time to get better structures and mindsets in place to do just that as we respond to what you will be putting into action. It is the school's job and responsibility to set the tone and create the space for parents to *be* champions—we both must hold up our ends of the partnership. It will be pressure for us, but a good kind of pressure. It is going to cause us to *be* different and to *do* different. For some, this is not a good thing, for others it's a great thing, and for our children—the ones who matter most in this—it is the best thing.

In order to transform our schools into the quality and successful institutions they are now intended to be, school operations must be more engaging and inclusive to everyone they serve. This level of engagement and change is going to be a transformational process, a process that may not always feel good or be smooth. It is going to be a paradigm shift in our ways of being in order to make these improvements from a place of compassion and love. To participate in this transformation fully will require us all to be willing and open to do that which we often to not want to do: be open to change and be open to feel discomfort. The transformation will require that we get uncomfortable, have difficult conversations, and be challenged to face ourselves. We must remember that we are on the same team with the same positive intent for our children. We must be mature and wise enough to trust the process with all of its uncertainty while keeping our focus: the greater success of our children.

As an educational leader fully supporting educational parenting, I humbly ask you to do two things:

1. Begin to put into action what you have read in this book *AND*
2. Be patient and compassionate with your children's school leaders and teachers as we work to better serve you and your children.

It is my hope that you have gleaned and identified next steps for yourself in regards to educational parenting and are now on your way to becoming a Parent Champion. Your first step is simple: take action where you are clear. Your spirit will not mislead you; you know what you must do to honor the educational experience of your child.

Overall Message From Chapter Eight

Please trust the process; this is going to take time.

Parent Champion Precepts:

1. Our schools need time to adjust to parents being partners and more involved.

2. The pressure of partnering must be a good, supportive, and compassionate pressure.

3. Partnering process may be hard, but that's okay because it is worth it for my child.

Next Level Action Agenda:

1. Put the Parent Champion strategies and tools to work.

2. Trust the process of transformation – for myself and my child's school.

3. Have compassion for my child's teachers and school leaders as well as for myself.

Thoughts & Reflections:

Peace and Blessings

RECOMMENDED RESOURCES

The following is a list of resources that I have found invaluable in the educational parenting journey. Of course, the age of your child and where you are on your own Parent Champion path will determine the usefulness of these resources.

- www.bigfuture.collegeboard.org ("Get Started" tab and then go to "For Parents")
- *A Middle School Plan for Students with College-Bound Dreams,* by Mychal Wynn
- *A High School Plan for Students with College-Bound Dreams,* by Mychal Wynn
- *Daring Greatly: How the Courage to Be Vulnerable Transforms the Way We Live, Love, Parent, and Lead,* by Brene Brown
- *Full Esteem Ahead: 100 Ways to Build Self-Esteem in Children and Adults,* by Diane Loomans and Julia Loomans
- *Skills I Wish I Learned in School: Building a Research Paper,* by Nicole Lusiani Elliott

- *I Will Teach You to Be Rich: No Guilt. No Excuses. No B.S. - Just a 6 Week Program That Works,* by Ramit Sethi
- *Life Visioning: A Transformative Process for Activating Your Unique Gifts and Highest Potential,* by Michael Bernard Beckwith
- *Mindset: The New Psychology of Success,* by Carol Dweck
- *The Price of Privilege: How Parental Pressure and Material Advantage Are Creating a Generation of Disconnected and Unhappy Kids,* by Madeline Levine PhD

ABOUT the AUTHOR

Tovi C. Scruggs is a visionary and innovative educator who serves as principal of San Lorenzo High School, where her career in education began 20 years ago. Returning to San Lorenzo High after co-founding her own private school (ASA Academy & Community Science Center) with 100% success rates, she brought a wealth of experience, skills, and talents to bring her beliefs and concepts about "best practices" to larger scale in public education.

In only one year under her leadership at SLz High, she and her team of teachers have created an academic culture, forged a redesign of campus climate that has resulted in restorative practices to reduce discipline referrals and suspension rates, and delved more deeply into issues of equity impacting academic achievement. Partnering with a group of like-minded parents, Tovi spearheaded the critical movement to establish the first PTSA at SLz High in over 20 years.

This journey of success began in a school-wide assembly where she simply told students what was true and what they needed to hear most: that she *loved* them.

Departing Los Angeles, CA where she was born and raised, Tovi earned two Bachelor of Arts degrees—in English and Social Welfare—from the University of California at Berkeley in 1993. She continued her education with graduate studies at Mills College, earning a secondary teaching credential in both English and Health and a Masters in Education, with an emphasis in teaching.

Tovi was honored as one of Black Expo's "101 Outstanding Women" in 2006 and as one of "101 Champions for Youth" in 2008. In 2011, another award followed with the 100 Black Men of the Bay Area's "Community Hero" Award. Tovi has served on numerous professional committees in leadership roles, conducted workshops at national conferences, and has delivered several keynotes to both adults and youth.

Continuing to nurture her love of growth and development for herself, leaders, and others, Tovi is a

Certified Integral Coach® by New Ventures West. She uses the methodology of integral coaching in her professional work with parents, teachers, and school administrators at all levels, focusing on leadership and lifestyle coaching that results in the transformation of mindsets and ways of being to positively impact our work with the children we serve.

Tovi continues to dream big, as she visions even greater success for those she serves.

"When I stand before God at the end of my life,
I would hope that I would not have a single bit of talent left,
and could say,
'I used everything You gave me."
—Erma Bombeck

To contact Tovi please visit www.ticiess.com

WORKSHOPS

Tovi Scruggs has education workshops for parents, families, teachers & educational leaders.

PARENTS & FAMILIES
Parent Champion Precepts

This workshop is designed to inspire parents to analyze, reflect, and take action in regards to how they co-educate and partner with their child's school. While schools are creating a culture of success, so too will families.

Building the Home-School Connection

Your child's best chance at academic and personal success is linked to the strength of the home-school connection. In this workshop, learn key methods, strategies, and structures to build a solid home-school connection and Parent Champion behaviors.

Designing a Balanced Summer

What does a healthy summer look like? Our students are not in traditional school for almost two months.

This requires a shift in family life as well as mind-set, habits, and structure. Don't let summer un-do all that you have put into place as a *Parent Champion*. Academic activities, personal growth, rest, and play are all key to building a balanced summer so you and your child can live balanced lives.

Back-to-School Readiness

Being ready for school is more than new clothes and new school supplies. Readiness is a growth mindset, the proper attitude, emotional stability, and the organizational structures in place to be ready to "do school" instead of letting another year of school do you.

Parents' Right to Choose: School Selection for Your Child

This workshop educates parents about the types of schools that exist, assists parents in getting clear about the best school for their child, and then guides parents in how to best select a school with clear step by step guidance.

TEACHERS & SCHOOL LEADERS

Creating an Academic School Culture

With tried and tested strategies, teachers and administrators will explore and learn the process for creating a more academic school culture as well as the specific methods and tools to build a strong academic culture.

Closing the Achievement Gap: Strategies to Effectively Teach African-American Students

Like all children, African-American students are extremely gifted and genius, yet most of the statistics do not reflect this. This workshop presents and delineates concrete methods and strategies to tap into that genius and create academic success.

An Educator's Mindset for Educational Parenting

This workshop is excellent for educators desiring to grow and learn in this area, especially those in teacher induction and administrative tier I and II programs. As schools embrace greater parent engagement, what mindsets and ways-of-being are critical to ensure growth and success in this area? This workshop will address the answer to that question, as well as provide a forum for the discussion of skills and strategies needed to support greater parent engagement.

Visioning Achievement: Spiritual Tools for Teaching and Leading

Learn steps and tools to embrace the "educator's lifestyle" with ease and flow. Designed for the spiritually-conscious educator of any age, explore and understand how spiritual tools and practices can be used to create greater work-life balance, more time in your day, more positive classroom/school climate, and improve student-achievement in order to fulfill your career and life aspirations to experience the life you envisioned.

PARENTS, FAMILIES, TEACHERS, & SCHOOL LEADERS

The Power of Vision & Visioning: Allowing, Being, & Creating

Vision is the physician. A clear vision can heal a situation, guide a mission, and/or allow you to consistently live from a place of clarity. Learn the power of vision as well as the practice of visioning to activate your vision from a place of inner-work and inner-preparation of be-ing that allows deep clarity before taking action. Often effortless, visioning allows you to embrace new ways-of-being and navigate internal shifts to manifesting and living the highest vision for your life. When your vision is clear, your decisions are easy.

Meditation 101

Meditation is a tool that allows you to connect to your own best teacher and source of wisdom – you. Embracing meditation as a practice to connect to our inner-voice of guidance, we will explore the simplistic precepts of beginning-level meditation both conceptually and experientially.

Crafting a Mission Statement for Your Life

Alignment of your words, actions, and thoughts is critical to success. By spending time focusing and crafting a written statement that speaks to how and why you live and lead, you will have a critical tool to govern your life from a place of purpose and integrity each day. You will write your personal roadmap to guide your daily choices, align your actions, and use the power of your word to manifest the life you desire.

Vision Boards & Creation Pages

Using our inner and outer creative selves, vision boards and creation pages are a tool to allow us to incorporate manifestation principles and/or all 3 forms of meditation simultaneously if used properly.

Creating from Flow

This workshop is designed with the intention of balancing work and relaxation to create the carefree life experience you dream of. Exploratory and experiential with a series of activities that result in a personalized roadmap of your professional and personal success that captures your vision and helps you get in the flow – an alignment of your desires, goals, actions, and results. In essence, you will learn to create from the flow of your spirit, honoring that flow to increase your time, productivity, joy, creativity, and success.

Conscious Creative Action: Living & Leading with Time & Spaciousness

Busy-ness is a distraction (a dis-attraction). Do you want to create more time in your life? Do you have projects and ideas you'd like to develop but don't have time or the discipline to move forward on your ideas and goals? Do you want to implement a deeper commitment of action to your life's purpose and work? This workshop will empower you to shift the trajectory of your life to step into action and create! In this workshop, you will learn about the new Creation Formula™ and other tried and true strategies to learn to create from the flow of life. The course uses a balance of practical tools & strategies along with spiritual tools (meditation, visioning, & Creation Pages™). At the end of this learning journey, you will have the tools to live your life more consciously and know how to take conscious creative action on your goals, projects, and dreams – and still have time to enjoy your life.

To contact Tovi about presenting at parent meetings/workshops, professional development for teachers and/or administrators, conferences, or coaching, please visit www.ticiess.com.

CPSIA information can be obtained at www.ICGtesting.com
Printed in the USA
LVOW01s1023090215

426259LV00016B/97/P